BOOK ANALYSIS

By Joe Burgis

Scoop
BY EVELYN WAUGH

Bright
≡Summaries.com

BOOK ANALYSIS

Shed new light on your favorite books with

Bright
≡Summaries.com

www.brightsummaries.com

EVELYN WAUGH	**9**
SCOOP	**13**
SUMMARY	**17**

The wrong Boot
To Ishmaelia
Expensive specimens
A new world
It's news
Counter-revolution
Boot is back

CHARACTER STUDY	**29**

William Boot
Mr Salter
Lord Copper
Mr Baldwin

ANALYSIS	**35**

"I ought to warn you that I am a journalist"
Town vs. country
"Comic extravaganza"

FURTHER REFLECTION	**45**
FURTHER READING	**49**

EVELYN WAUGH

ENGLISH WRITER

- **Born in London in 1903.**
- **Died in Somerset in 1966.**
- **Notable works:**
  - *Decline and Fall* (1928), novel
  - *A Handful of Dust* (1934), novel
  - *Brideshead Revisited* (1945), novel

Evelyn Waugh was an English novelist and journalist. He was educated at Lancing College, Sussex and later earned a third-class degree from Hertford College, Oxford. After working as a schoolmaster, briefly attending art school, taking carpentry lessons and attempting to drown himself only to be put off by a jellyfish, he published his first book, a biography of the artist Dante Gabriel Rossetti, in 1928, and his first novel, *Decline and Fall*, later that year. There followed a conversion to Roman Catholicism in 1930, a second marriage in 1937, the births of seven children, journeys in Africa and South America, stints in the Royal Marines, the Commandos and the

Special Service Brigade during the Second World War and the publication of 13 more novels and several works of non-fiction, before his death on Easter Sunday in 1966. Waugh is revered as one of English literature's finest prose stylists and fiercest satirists. His greatest novels are typically both hilarious and disturbing and chronicle the chaos, disillusionment and moral ambiguity of the years between the two World Wars.

SCOOP

A NOVEL ABOUT JOURNALISTS

- **Genre:** novel
- **Reference edition:** Waugh, E. (2000) *Scoop*. [Ebook]. London: Penguin Classics.
- **1st edition:** 1938
- **Themes:** journalism, news, politics, war, country life

Scoop was Evelyn Waugh's fifth novel. Published in 1938 and described in a *New York Times* review as "uproariously funny" (*The New York Times*, 1938), it is a thrilling and farcical portrait of life as a foreign correspondent.

The unsuspecting William Boot – country gentleman and nature columnist – is plucked from obscurity by Lord Copper, the omnipotent owner of the *Daily Beast*, and dispatched to Ishmaelia in Africa, where war is brewing. "Best of luck" he is told. "We shall expect the first victory about the beginning of July" (p. 56).

Largely uninterested in his trade and entirely ignorant of the Ishmaelite situation, Boot nonetheless manages – quite by accident and under the noses of his vastly more experienced colleagues – to uncover a major story, much to the delight of all back at the *Beast*.

By the time *Scoop* was published, Waugh was already established as one of the pre-eminent novelists of the age. The novel remains a favourite among his readers, and is held by journalists to be one of the finest fictional portrayals of their profession in English literature.

SUMMARY

THE WRONG BOOT

John Courtney Boot – successful novelist and travel writer – visits Mrs Stitch – wife of the cabinet minister Algernon Stitch – to ask a favour. Intent on escaping an unfortunate romance, John asks Mrs Stitch to use her influence to arrange for him to be sent as a foreign correspondent to Ishmaelia in Africa, where war is rumoured to be imminent. Mrs Stitch duly lunches with Lord Copper, head of the Megalopolitan Corporation and overseer of the *Daily Beast*, who happens to be short of a foreign correspondent after an unhappy dispute over the exact date of the Battle of Hastings. Mrs Stitch works her magic and Lord Copper makes his wishes known to his foreign editor, Mr Salter: "I tell you who I want: Boot" (p. 18). Unsure of exactly who Boot is, Mr Salter flicks through a copy of the *Beast* and finds that a man of that very name – William Boot – writes the nature column.

William Boot lives at Boot Magna Hall, along with his sister Priscilla, his uncle Theodore, his uncle Roderick, his great-aunt Anne, his uncle Bernard, his widowed mother and grandmother and Nannie Bloggs. He is devoted to writing his nature column, *Lush Places*, but has come to fear for his job after his sister, Priscilla, sabotaged his latest effort by substituting the words "great-crested grebe" for the word "badger" throughout it (p. 25). When he receives a telegram from Mr Salter summoning him to London, he expects the worst. However, Mr Salter explains that Lord Copper is an admirer and wants William to travel to Ishmaelia to cover the war. At first William declines the offer, until Mr Salter politely explains that if he refuses, he will be sacked: "Lord Copper expects his staff to work wherever the best interests of the paper call them" (p. 45).

TO ISHMAELIA

William is kitted out for his mission. He acquires:

> "[A] tent, three months' rations, a collapsible canoe, a jointed flagstaff and Union Jack, a hand-pump and sterilizing plant, an astrolabe, six suits of tropical linen and a sou'wester, a camp operating table and set of surgical instruments,

> a portable humidor, guaranteed to preserve cigars in condition in the Red Sea, and a Christmas hamper complete with Santa Claus costume and a tripod mistletoe stand, and a cane for whacking snakes" (pp. 58-59).

Without a passport, however, his departure is delayed.

Eventually underway, William first flies to Paris. On board the plane he meets an important looking man – "neatly, rather stiffly dressed for the time of year, and heavily jewelled" (p. 72). The man makes an impression on William, though his name remains a mystery, even after the two meet again on the train to Marseilles. On the boat bound for Africa, William meets Corker, a fellow journalist, who takes William under his wing: "You know, you've got a lot to learn about journalism. Look at it this way. News is what a chap who doesn't much care about anything wants to read. And it's only news until he's read it. After that it's dead" (p. 88).

Back in London, John Courtney Boot seeks out Mrs Stitch and asks to know what came of her efforts to help him. His chagrin is particularly acute as he has already staged an emotional goodbye to his troublesome lover. Mrs Stitch is bemused.

EXPENSIVE SPECIMENS

Mrs Earl Russell Jackson's Hotel in Jacksonburg, Ishmaelia, is heaving with journalists, including William, Corker and the formidable Sir Jocelyn Hitchcock, whose apparent disappearance is construed to mean that he is on to that most precious of things – a story – though in fact he is holed up in an annexe 50 yards away. Another journalist, Shumble, produces a story about a Russian agent, much to his jealous colleagues' displeasure, but it is not long before the story dies when it is publicly denied by Dr Benito, Minister of Foreign Affairs and Propaganda. William finds that an old school friend, Jack Bannister, is the Vice-Consul in Ishmaelia. They arrange to have dinner. Bannister informs William that there is "something rather odd going on" in the country and that there was some truth to Shumble's story about Russian influence (p. 134). William, in possession of this knowledge, begins to enjoy the thrill of the journalistic chase: "he saw his name figuring in future history books" (p. 136). Corker soon rids him of his delusions, however: "No one's going to print your story after the way it's been denied. Russian agents are off the menu, brother" (p. 137).

William and Corker move to another hotel, the Pension Dressler, where William meets Kätchen, who is awaiting the return of her husband and looking after a bag of stones – "specimens" – for him (p. 152). One thing leads to another and together they erect William's collapsible canoe in his hotel room and sit in it, knees touching, before Corker interrupts: "Not bad, brother, not bad at all. I will say you're a quick worker" (p. 156). William, enamoured, agrees to buy the stones for £20, as Kätchen has been left without means.

Word spreads that Sir Jocelyn Hitchcock is at the fascist headquarters in the interior of the country and all the other journalists rush to follow him there. William, however, is instructed not to go by the *Beast*, where Mr Salter is growing increasingly troubled by the lack of stories their new man is producing.

A NEW WORLD

Kätchen and William drive into the hills together. "Kätchen, I love you. Darling Kätchen, I love you" William announces (p. 172). Sir Jocelyn Hitchcock, who never really left, emerges from his hotel room and prepares to depart. "CONSIDER ISHMAELITE STORY UP-CLEANED" he informs his employer (*ibid.*). William is left as the only special correspondent in Jacksonburg.

He and Kätchen fall out because he keeps saying he loves her and she, for now, is loyal to her husband. The next day William establishes that her husband is not really her husband because he already has another wife. Meanwhile, Corker and fellow correspondent Pigge get stuck in a lorry on the outskirts of town. William goes to see Bannister, who suggests there might be action in Jacksonburg soon: "look out for that Russian I told you about and watch your friend Dr Benito" (p. 186). Back in London, Salter reacts badly to a rare telegram from William: "RATHER ENJOYING THINGS WEATHER IMPROVING" (p. 187). Kätchen offers to help William find some news after he receives a number of angry telegrams from the *Beast*. William reiterates his love for her, at which Kätchen mellows and concedes that her husband has perhaps treated her rather badly. They go to bed.

After more than two decades of celibacy, the evening makes quite an impression on our hero: "Next morning William awoke in a new world" (p. 193).

IT'S NEWS

Kätchen makes good on her offer to help and uncovers some actual news: President Jackson has been imprisoned for the last four days. William immediately wires this to the *Beast*, but before it is received in London, he discovers he has been sacked. Unperturbed, he attends a tea party given by Bannister, where Dr Benito makes every effort to persuade him to leave Jacksonburg and join his floundering colleagues in the interior. William refuses, returns to his hotel, discovers his contract has been "unterminated" (p. 206) and learns that Kätchen has been abducted by soldiers. A representative of Dr Benito comes to buy the "specimens", but William refuses. He takes them to Bannister for safekeeping, who identifies them as gold ore.

William puts together everything he has discovered and sends it to London:

> "The general editor looked. He saw *'Russian plot… coup d'etat … overthrow constitutional government … red dictatorship … goat butts head of police … imprisoned blonde … vital British interest jeopardized,'* it was enough; it was news. 'It's news,' he said… 'Stop the machines […] Scrap the whole front page.'" (pp. 210-211).

Even Mr Salter acknowledges William's stunning success: "Lord Copper knew best" he concedes (p. 212).

COUNTER-REVOLUTION

Back at his hotel, William is disturbed by the arrival of Kätchen's husband, who explains he was involved with rival presidential candidate, the fascist usurper Mr Smiles Soum. It becomes clear that all members of the ruling family – the Jacksons – are being arrested by the ascendant communists. Kätchen is freed and she and William agree to marry, until William leads her to her husband and she swiftly changes her mind. "William, you are not jealous? How I despise jealousy" (p. 218). Kätchen and her husband promptly escape using William's collapsible canoe and William, a little sore, returns to the city to find the communists have taken over. Just as the chaos seems to be reaching its peak, William's mysterious friend, his bejewelled travelling companion, descends upon the scene in a parachute.

Mr Baldwin is the man's alias. "It is a convenient name" he explains (p. 226). Following the triumph of the communists, Jacksonburg has been renamed Marxville. The shadowy Mr Baldwin gives William the lowdown on Ishmaelia:

"It's all very simple. There has been competition for the mineral rights of Ishmaelia which, I may say as their owner, have been preposterously overvalued" (pp. 231-232).

The German and Russian governments have been vying for influence in the country to secure access to its wealth.

Dr Benito appears and launches into a long, Marxist speech, but is soon shooed away by supporters of President Jackson, who is duly reinstated after having been liberated from a garden shed. "I think we may be satisfied that the counter-revolution has triumphed" concludes Mr Baldwin (p. 239). He then writes a message to the *Beast* on William's behalf, securing him a momentous scoop and eternal journalistic glory.

BOOT IS BACK

In London, Lord Copper decides that William ought to receive a knighthood. John Courtney Boot is promptly informed that he is to be so honoured and Mrs Stitch takes credit: "I suppose I did have something to do with it [...] Just the Stitch service" (p. 251).

Returning home, William realises he is famous. The front page of the *Beast* bears the headline: "BOOT IS BACK" (p. 252). Though eagerly awaited at the *Beast*'s offices, he slips away back to Boot Magna. Despite the wishes of the great Lord Copper, William refuses to attend the banquet at which his misplaced knighthood is to be celebrated, as well as an extremely lucrative contract. He wishes only to resume his work on *Lush Places*.

Intent on persuading the *Beast*'s new star otherwise, Mr Salter travels to Boot Magna.

The London man finds this rare venture into rural climes fantastically unpleasant: "Cattle had closed silently in on him [...] dogs had flown at him in three farmyards [...] he had tumbled through an overgrown stile" (p. 274). The Boots deduce that he must be an alcoholic and deny him all drink at dinner. William cannot be made to attend the banquet, but agrees to sign a contract, believing it to be an invitation to continue filing *Lush Places*.

And yet Mr Salter still has a problem: Lord Copper must not be disappointed. A Boot must attend the banquet. Uncle Theodore steps into the breach and behaves so objectionably that Mr Salter is threatened with the sack.

The story closes with Mr Salter as Art Editor of *Home Knitting*, Sir John Boot in the Antarctic and William comfortably re-installed at Boot Magna, just about ready for bed.

CHARACTER STUDY

WILLIAM BOOT

William Boot lives in Boot Magna Hall with several members of his family. In addition to looking after his estate, he is employed as the author of *Lush Places* – a nature column – by the *Daily Beast*. "The work was of the utmost importance to him: he was paid a guinea at a time and it gave him the best possible excuse for remaining uninterruptedly in the country" (p. 25). Mistaken for the renowned writer John Courtney Boot (a distant cousin), William is ordered by the *Beast* to go to Ishmaelia and report on the impending war. Though deeply reluctant to go, he makes a fantastic, and unexpected, success of his mission. Ultimately, his good manners, good luck, cheerful amateurism and occasionally firm hand see him win the day. Like many of Waugh's heroes, he fills the role accidentally; unlike some, he is allowed to triumph. Since the novel was published, William Boot has been immortalised as the archetypal blundering yet well-meaning foreign correspondent. He wears his success endearingly lightly, preferring to return as soon as possible to the quiet life at Boot Magna after his exploits, and declining Lord Copper's invitation to a lavish banquet given in his honour.

MR SALTER

Mr Salter was happy as the editor of the Woman's Page, and happier still when, prior to that, "he had chosen the jokes for one of Lord Copper's little weeklies" (p. 17). Unfortunately for him, "it was the policy of the Megalopolitan to keep the staff alert by constant changes of occupation" (*ibid*.). Thus, it is as the *Beast*'s Foreign Editor that we encounter him. He has learned to deal tactfully with his formidable employer:

> "Mr Salter's side of the conversation was limited to expressions of assent. When Lord Copper was right, he said 'Definitely, Lord Copper'; when he was wrong, 'Up to a point.'
> 'Let me see, what's the name of the place I mean? Capital of Japan? Yokohama, isn't it?'
> 'Up to a point, Lord Copper.'
> 'And Hong Kong belongs to us now, doesn't it?'
> 'Definitely, Lord Copper'" (p. 17).

Mr Salter is anxious when William fails to send any news for a prolonged period. Ultimately though, he is forced to acknowledge Lord Copper's brilliant judgement: "Lord Copper knew best" (p. 212). At Lord Copper's insistence, Mr Salter travels to the countryside to persuade William to remain at the *Beast*. It is a miserable visit and his suspicions as to the hideousness of country life are confirmed. In the end he finds satisfaction, taking on a job as "Art Editor of *Home Knitting*" (p. 303).

LORD COPPER

"Towering above the journalists who throng the story is the newspaper magnate Lord Copper" Waugh's biographer Christopher Sykes writes, "an imaginary portrait (by Evelyn's own admission) of Lord Beaverbrook, whom Evelyn had met, served under spasmodically, but never came to know" (Sykes, 1975: 247). Lord Beaverbrook was a newspaper publisher and politically influential in the early 20th century. In *Scoop*, as Sykes puts it, he appears to suffer from "megalomania bordering on insanity" (*ibid*.). He is persuaded to hire John Courtney Boot by the charming Mrs Stitch, but thanks to Mr Salter's blunder, William Boot is recruited instead. Lord Copper, of course, takes credit for this triumph, recommends William for a knighthood and throws a banquet in his honour.

> "Lord Copper quite often gave banquets; it would be an understatement to say that no one enjoyed them more than the host for no one else enjoyed them at all, while Lord Copper positively exalted in every minute" (p. 294).

MR BALDWIN

Mr Baldwin is the enigmatic figure upon whom the entire Ishmaelite drama seems to hinge. In courteously offering Mr Baldwin a seat on an aeroplane, William secures his good opinion and, ultimately, inadvertently, the scoop that will make him famous. Sykes describes Mr Baldwin as "the sinister leading character with purple-dyed hair who is represented as a person of indeterminate nationality, superhuman ability and grotesque dishonesty" (Sykes: 246).

Having arrived on the scene in Jacksonburg (briefly Marxville) by parachute, Mr Baldwin explains his involvement to William: "It is all very simple. There has been competition for the mineral rights of Ishmaelia which, I may say as their owner, have been preposterously overvalued" (p. 232). It is for this reason that Mr Baldwin holds sway over the rival factions, both domestic and international, that are attempting to seize control of the country.

ANALYSIS

"I OUGHT TO WARN YOU THAT I AM A JOURNALIST"

W. F. Deedes, formerly editor of the *Daily Telegraph* and held by some to be the model for William Boot, explains that Evelyn Waugh's career as a journalist was not a great success: at the *Daily Express*, "Waugh had worked briefly as a probationer in 1927 before getting the sack. (He had not proved one of their "discoveries". Only one piece he wrote appeared in the paper - and that was alleged to have been stolen from another newspaper - and after five weeks, he was out)" (*The Telegraph*, 2003).

In *Scoop*, Waugh seems at once disparaging and admiring of the profession. There is certainly some relish for correspondents' camaraderie, though not all of Boot's colleagues are drawn sympathetically. As Sykes writes, "one of Evelyn's most horrific portraits" is of William's mentor Corker, "the quintessential vulturous foreign correspondent" (Sykes: 248). While Corker generously volunteers his expertise to help William, his cynicism abounds: "They gave Jakes the Nobel Peace Prize for his harrowing descriptions of the carnage - but that was colour stuff" (p. 91). The pursuit of news appears to bring out the worst in people: Shumble – one of the journalists installed at the same hotel as William – having had the gall to file a story without tipping off his fellows, "sat in the lounge radiating importance. Throughout the evening everyone in turn sat by his side, offered him whisky and casually reminded him of past acts of generosity" (p. 119).

There are moments when the scales seem to tip definitively towards disparagement: "Shumble, Whelper and Pigge knew Corker; they had loitered together of old on many a doorstep and forced an entry into many a stricken home" (p. 114).

But Sykes reports a revealing admission: Waugh, having travelled to Abyssinia (now Ethiopia) to write journalism and travel pieces, explains that his "ordeals" were "not a waste of time". He goes on: "On Thursday 15th made very good start with the first pages of a novel" (Sykes: 237). The novel was *Scoop*.

Compare this with Mr Baldwin's assessment of journalistic writing in general:

> "I read the newspapers with lively interest. It is seldom that they are absolutely, point-blank wrong. That is the popular belief, but those who are in the know can usually discern an embryo of truth, a little grit of fact, like the core of a pearl, round which have been deposited the delicate layers of ornament" (p. 230).

Perhaps it is because *Scoop* is based on actual experiences of journalism – that 'embryo of truth' – that the reader's impression is, ultimately, that Waugh harbours some real affection for the trade, even while he satirizes it so mercilessly. For a novelist who so often drew on real life and real people for inspiration, it is arguable that Waugh's fictional craft is imbued with certain journalistic qualities.

As in much of Waugh's work, it is difficult to establish whether he takes any views on the subject. He seems to have been largely averse to taking views, preferring instead to create polished works of fiction. What he describes in his preface as a "light hearted tale" (p. v) may be taken as exactly that – a story without particularly serious satirical motives. Waugh always considered himself, first and foremost, a literary craftsman, and this is as evident in *Scoop* as anywhere else. As Sykes puts it: "The story is as complicated as the most sophisticated French or English eighteenth-century farce" (Sykes: 247).

TOWN VS. COUNTRY

Country houses appear in almost all of Waugh's novels. He spent a lot of time in them and many of his friends lived in them. In *Scoop*, we are invited into Boot Magna Hall, home to William Boot and eight other members of his family. To Waugh, the country house represented not only a crowning architectural achievement, but also a way of life that he revered and saw was fading. It is telling that Sykes reports, after the publication of *Scoop*, Waugh "became greatly preoccupied with the garden at Piers Court" and was beginning to live "the country gentleman's life":

> "He began for the moment to forget the delights of London, but he never took a deep pleasure in country life, even though he was experiencing it under ideal conditions: with a wife with whom he was passionately in love and in a charming

> and elegant country house in a lovely countryside." (Sykes: 251)

This tension between town and country living is mined to great comic effect in *Scoop*. With typical symmetrical precision, Waugh brings the country to the town at the beginning of the novel (as William travels up to London, expecting to be reprimanded by his superiors at the *Beast*) and the town to the country at the end (as Mr Salter ventures to Boot Magna to secure William's services and ward off advances from a rival paper, the *Brute*).

William's trip to London begins badly. "His spirits began to sink; the mood of defiance passed. It was always the way; the moment he left the confines of Boot Magna he found himself in a foreign and hostile world" (p. 30). And it does not improve: "At seven he reached Paddington and the atrocious city was all around him" (*ibid*.).

By contrast, Mr Salter is a city man, through and through:

> "'The country', for him, meant what you saw in the train between Liverpool Street and Frinton. If a psycho-analyst, testing his associations, had

> suddenly said to Mr Salter the word 'farm', the surprising response would have been 'Bang', for he had once been blown up and buried while sheltering in a farm in Flanders... there was something unEnglish and not quite right about 'the country', with its solitude and self-sufficiency." (pp. 33-34)

His eventual encounter with 'the country' confirms him in his attitudes. He is forced to contend not only with the immense physical discomfort it causes, but also with the manners of the people that inhabit it:

> "He stood under the porch, sweating, blistered, nettle-stung, breathless, parched, dizzy, deadbeat and dishevelled, with his bowler hat in one hand and umbrella in the other, leaning against a stucco pillar waiting for someone to open the door. Nobody came" (pp. 274-275).

The two worlds are thoroughly incompatible, and Waugh belonged to them both. In *Scoop*, they collide, with brilliantly comic consequences. In other novels, notably *A Handful of Dust*, the collision is rather more tragic. It is a testament to his skills as a craftsman, and his originality as a stylist, that Waugh was able to deploy his experiences of these worlds to such radically different ends, and to capture them both with such verve.

"COMIC EXTRAVAGANZA"

The novel was well received when it was published in 1938. Sykes tells us: "*Scoop* was justly acclaimed, and those who declared it to be one of Evelyn's best books which would long be remembered were wholly justified" (Sykes: 248).

Robert Van Gelder reviewed it very favourably in the *New York Times* at the time of publication: "With this book England's wittiest novelist sets a new standard for comic extravaganza. This novel reads as though it had been formed with a slapstick but given its final shaping with a lancet" (*New York Times*, 1938).

And the novel continues to acquire admirers. Interviewed by the same paper, the spy writer Ben Macintyre (bestselling British author of *The Spy and the Traitor* [2018], born in 1963), when asked which book by another author he wishes he had written, replied:

"I would love to have written *Scoop* by Evelyn Waugh, that vicious but affectionate satire of journalism, exposing our trade in all its insane competitiveness, bravery, inefficiency and strange nobility. I must have read it a dozen times, and it still makes me snort" (*New York Times*, 2018).

FURTHER REFLECTION

SOME QUESTIONS TO THINK ABOUT...

- How is Waugh's style different to that of other authors?
- To what extent is Waugh's satire of journalists and newspapers relevant today? Do you see any parallels with the modern media?
- What, if any, political preoccupations do you detect in the novel?
- Do you think Waugh admires or dislikes journalism and journalists? Why?
- Can you think of other novels with accidental heroes? How do they compare to *Scoop*?
- Do you think a divide persists between town and country dwellers in Britain today? In what ways are the two lifestyles still different?
- Are you sceptical about the factual accuracy of the news you consume? Why?

We want to hear from you!
Leave a comment on your online library
and share your favourite books on social media!

FURTHER READING

REFERENCE EDITION

- Waugh, E. (2000) *Scoop*. [Ebook]. London: Penguin Classics.

REFERENCE STUDIES

- (2018) By the Book: Ben Macintyre. *The New York Times*. [Online]. [Accessed 11 November 2018]. Available from: <https://www.nytimes.com/2018/08/30/books/review/by-the-book-ben-macintyre.html>
- Deeds, W. F. (2003) The Real Scoop: Who Was Who in Waugh's Cast List and Why. *The Telegraph*. [Online]. [Accessed 11 November 2018]. Available from: <https://www.telegraph.co.uk/culture/donotmigrate/3595475/The-real-Scoop-who-was-who-in-Waughs-cast-list-and-why.html>
- Sykes, C. (1975) *Evelyn Waugh: A Biography*. London: Penguin Books.
- Van Gelder, R. (1938) A New Standard for Comic Extravaganza. *The New York Times*. [Online]. [Accessed 11 November 2018]. Available from: <http://movies2.nytimes.com/books/99/10/10/specials/waugh-scoop.html>

ADDITIONAL SOURCES

- Stannard, M. (1990) *Evelyn Waugh: The Early Years, 1903-1939*. London: W. W. Norton & Company.
- Waugh, E. Davie, M. ed. (1979) *The Diaries of Evelyn Waugh: 1911-1965*. London: Penguin Books.

ADAPTATIONS

- *Scoop.* (1987) [TV Film]. Gavin Millar. Dir. UK: London Weekend Television.

MORE FROM BRIGHTSUMMARIES.COM

- Reading guide – *Decline and Fall* by Evelyn Waugh.
- Reading guide – *Vile Bodies* by Evelyn Waugh.

Bright≡Summaries.com

BOOK ANALYSIS

More guides to rediscover your love of literature

- *Animal Farm* by George Orwell
- *The Stranger* by Albert Camus
- *Harry Potter and the Sorcerer's Stone* by J.K. Rowling
- *The Silence of the Sea* by Vercors
- *Antigone* by Jean Anouilh
- *The Flowers of Evil* by Baudelaire

www.brightsummaries.com

Although the editor makes every effort to verify the accuracy of the information published, BrightSummaries.com accepts no responsibility for the content of this book.

© BrightSummaries.com, 2019. All rights reserved.

www.brightsummaries.com

Ebook EAN: 9782808015592

Paperback EAN: 9782808015608

Legal Deposit: D/2018/12603/538

Cover: © Primento

Digital conception by Primento, the digital partner of publishers.